your tulip
SUNSHINE
RAYS OF POETRY

VAISHNAVI
VISWANATHAN

notionpress.com

INDIA • SINGAPORE • MALAYSIA

ISBN 979-8-88772-971-8

With remembrance of Appa

Contents

Acknowledgments

A book wouldn't exist without a reader. Thanks to all my readers.

Thanks to my family, without them nothing would have been possible.

Thanks to my best friend, who I call Dad, "S. Gautami", for always being behind my back and pushing forward. You have always been a well-wisher, guide and a very supportive supporter. Thanks for editing, advising and being my guide.

Thanks to Sai Tharun, for giving honest comments and being my personal editor.

Thanks to my senior Nachiyappan, my juniors Siddarth and Ishan for reviewing and sharing opinions. You guys have been a biggest support.

Thanks to my gang: Madhu Sri (Apple), Raasitha (Ranguskhi) and Manjima (Manji Mom), for tolerating, motivating, irritating and supporting.

Thanks to the Notion Press publication for getting me on board and for being as sweet as sugar throughout the publication process and also for boosting my excitement in each and every step.

"If not for you all, I wouldn't be here,
 I wouldn't be where I am now."

I thank each one of you whole heartedly
and I owe you all a lot.

I am sure that I would make you all proud one day.

This book belongs to each one of you.

Keep supporting, keep motivating
and keep blessing me.

Thank you.

To Appa

I sit down to write about you

And look back how far

I have traveled.

With and without you.

Through the path,

I see me being you.

And eventually,

I see you in me.

Expressive, bold, voicing out

Energetic and real.

I have traveled.

With and without you.

I want to call myself

"Father's princess,"

But I feel proud to be called

"Father's daughter."

Through the path,

I don't find moments with you.

But all I find is: people telling me:

You are him.

And that smile

That blooms in me

Is what makes

Me run.

Though you've gone too soon,

You haven't gone too far.

The way I'm honored now,

Is your honor.

I was the apple of your eye

And you were my apple pie.

Your majesty,

All you should realize is,

Your creation is amazingly yours here.

To Ayya

When I lost the hand that had to

Hold me tight,

I got you,

Holding me so tight.

So tall and vibrant you are,

As serenity of the sea.

Your kindness and love,

Reflection of the skies.

When you look my way, I feel so loved.

Walking with you, I feel beloved.

As a little girl, I follow your steps.

As a matured girl, I follow your theories.

With you beside me,

With I, beside you,

I have come a long way.

With all the learnings and unlearning.

Your answers to all my questions,

Weird ones too!

You working hard to bring me here,

Right where I'm right now.

Regardless of an extra mile every time,

Regardless of an extra piece of love,

Regardless of last-minute askings,

Regardless of last-minute plans.

Is what makes me.

For whatever I'm right now,

And I would be in few years.

Always your grandchild.

I stand with pride and dignity,

With love and protection.

A simple man

You are.

Lending a shoulder,

To ease the tears.

Holding a lamp high,

To bid bye to the fears.

Your smile,

An encouragement.

Your guidance and advice,

A motivation.

Your abundant advice,

A free philosophy and theory.

Your glory, the truth.

Our hero you are.

Always your proud grandchild.

Preface

Over the years, a lot of words, sentences and lines have been used by various poets and philosophers, trying to define poetry and its place in society and in humanity. All of them, while defining poetry and talking of what poetry means to that specific person, do not encompass the vast multitudes of poetry and all its meanings. As humans, we try to find what poetry is, what life is and how both are interwoven. This is Vaishnavi's attempt, unapologetic and real. This is the poetry of her life, of her dreams. Her thoughts, about nature, about life and everything else she could think of are condensed here, into these poems. These are her ways of remembrance, of curiosity and of immortalizing the beauty surrounding us. — Gautami. S

Live the Moment

Between the stars and moon

Which one shines bright? – questioned

A random old man

At a random roadside.

Amidst an aesthetic view around,

With a calm ground.

In between the prevailing silence,

Losing my sense.

I glared at him

And then looked away to pass by him.

He smirked

And sat alone on a stone-bench there.

He was staring at the sky,

I stalked him,

From afar.

He stared on – without a blink.

The random stranger,

Seemed strange.

But his stare,

Stole a piece of my heart.

His way of looking at the vast sky,

Urged me to look at it too,

And think

"Which one shines brighter?"

We were staring

For about an hour.

Yet, I couldn't

Conclude anything.

Losing my patience,

I stepped close to him,

He smirked

And I asked – "Why?"

He smirked again

And replied,

"I know you'll come back."

And that confused me.

"I came for..." – I continued

He interrupted me midsentence.

"For the answer."

And I nod.

He started his theory,

With the voice of wise and old.

"Perspectives are meant to be different.

What I see, isn't the same as you.

At times people admire,

Just the beauty of the moon.

At times people get mesmerized,

Just by the twinkle of the stars.

At times people praise,

The whole night.

At times people,

Just sleep.

But moon and stars don't stay long

Without each other's company.

Every fortnight, the moon

Bids its goodbye – to the stars.

In those lonely nights, stars don't shine.

They just twinkle!

Ever so small.

But still enrapture us."

"And now answer,

Which one shines brighter?" – He asked

And I stood there, answerless.

As he concluded.

"Certain questions,

Certain doubts,

Certain longings

Don't require an answer."

The Unstuck Scenery

Occasionally,

Heart beats faster,

Yet, the scene is the same,

And ain't lame.

The fragile flower sheds,

And a new one blossoms,

Yet, the scene is the same,

And ain't lame.

The sunshade rests a while,

And the dark clouds pour,

Yet, the scene is the same,

And ain't lame.

The butterflies fly,

And the sky so plain,

Yet, the scene is same,

And ain't lame.

The heart loves to trick,

And the soul too naïve.

Yet, the scene ain't same,

But not too lame.

A Bliss of Eternity

Between the curtains

A magical door,

Behind the door

A magical place,

With the slides.

After the door

The magical path,

With curvy handles

And architects' flavor.

Where do they lead to?

People perplex,

Some fail to flex,

Flex to different perspective.

Perspective.

Yeah!

Curtains – A satin wavy cloth,

That floats in the air.

Sliding doors – the smooth straight slide,

That glides with the flow.

Magical path – the space to the recreational world

That sways the mind.

Those curvy handles – the design that compliments
the scene.

They together lead to the magic of the nature,

The *maya* of the God,

Not being a theist,

Nor an atheist.

Yet, awe of the magic of the creator.

Creator's creation,

Magician's magic,

Mayas mayai,

Beautician's beauty.

The sun's ray,

A ray of hope,

A ray of Vitamin D,

A ray of bliss.

The moons twilight,

Twilight of romance,

Twilight of ecstasy,

Twilight of bliss.

The path that leads to the bliss,

A bliss of eternity.

Lost Garden

As I stepped,

Amidst the tulips and daffodils,

Which one should I admire?

The golden daffodils or

The red tulips.

The greens below them

Sweeping my tender feet,

The aura tickling at my nose,

The natural world,

Making me dream.

Dream

From the top,

With the sun's glow,

Illuminating the beauty,

As the rays spread.

The paths brightened,

The flowers bloomed,

Bees surrounded,

The long farmhouse,

With brick red shed.

With the view,

My heart skipping a beat,

The soul dreaming about a simple life,

Gazing at the farmhouse.

From a far distance.

It's a long-lost garden,

In the valley,

Midst of colors,

Thin line between the sky and ground.

A simple yet a beautiful journey of naturalism.

Remembrance

Travel with the nature,

Trek between the mountains,

Into the water,

Creating your own paths.

Sculpt your soul's peace,

Carve your happiness,

Flaunt your messy hair,

Admire your muddy legs.

Light the way you pass through,

Collect the shiny stones at the trail,

Walk at the random routes,

Cherish the journey.

Snap through your eyes

The best moments;

Watch through your eyes

The forever remembrance.

Race of Right

Between the stars and the moon,

Through the beam,

Under the shade,

With one petal.

Between the flowers and the bees,

Through the valley,

Under the sky,

With one tear.

Between the aura and the vibe,

Through the light,

Under the weight,

With one hope.

Stood the soul,

With fiery eye,

To win the race,

Race of right.

Heaven on Earth

Along the path of heaven,

With twists and turns,

At the sides

All a traveler could see – is beauty.

Beauty of the world,

Aesthetics of the synthetic,

Creative nature,

The dream of the longers.

The never-ending paths,

The paths between the growths,

The growths of the seeds,

The seeds that nurture.

Down the trail,

Through the paths of green,

At the sides

All a traveler could feel – is beauty

The beauty of the world,

The aesthetics of the synthetic,

The dream of the longers,

The heaven on earth.

A Simple Smile

A broken cottage,

With one table!

Half cracked

Old bricked shed.

Door half open,

Half-built steps

Below the door,

The plain lawn.

Surrounded by greens.

With flowers around

The broken cottage,

A modern building at a distance.

Perfectly constructed,

With terrace and balcony,

Designed space

Filled with furniture.

Road before the home,

Humans stressed,

Children tensed.

A sad modern life.

An old man before the cottage,

Watering the plants,

With birds around him.

Looks at the sun with a smile.

Walking with a stick,

At the broken cottage,

He showers and smiles,

A simple happy life.

A Little One

In the midst of sky and blue,

Between the ray and hue,

She's a little one,

Roaming to have fun.

In the midst of leaves and green,

Between the peace and scream,

She's a little one,

Peeping out to have fun.

In the midst of grass and flowers,

Between the trunks and barks,

She's a little one,

Riding and having fun.

In the midst of hot and chill,

Between the sun and rain,

She's a little one,

Swirling and relishing.

In the midst of fresh and sweat,

Between the traffic and rush,

She's a little one,

Dreaming and smiling.

The Parenting

Between the garlands of love,

Swings the glory

Of a little kid.

To and fro,

Swaying with the wind.

With the sweat,

Swings more.

And laughs more

The little kid.

Like no tomorrow.

When,

She is done,

She jumps down

With the sway of the swing

And runs down the lane

Into the field,

And churns

With the pure wind.

And laughs more with pebbles,

Like no tomorrow.

With her run,

Runs her mother

Along her side

To lift her up,

And hug her tight.

With the kid,

Laughs the mother

And smooches her tight

Like no tomorrow.

With the kid.

With the kid

Lies the happiness,

Of the mother.

Tight around her arms,

The kid relishes.

Stopped by the Wood

Stopped by the wood,

Creeped by the haunt,

At the edge of the bark,

It was twelve o'clock.

The creamy moon,

At the dreamy night,

At the edge of the bark

Seemed to be the ghost house.

The glossy cloud,

At the dreamy night,

At the edge of the bark,

Seemed to be the broken glass.

Stopped by the wood,

Creeped by the haunt.

At the edge of the bark

It was twelve o'clock.

Sharp bottles scattered down,

Down the lane.

Bottles and ashes filling

The clean lake.

Flowers and happiness,

Freshness and purity

Sinking at the lake,

A once clean lake.

Stopped by the wood,

It was twelve o'clock.

The creamy moon,

The glossy cloud.

The small kid,

Running a long way,

With no way now,

Stopped by the wood.

Creeped by the haunt,

At the edge of the bark,

With no way down

Stands the poor kid.

Scared and terrified,

No way down,

Down the lane,

Stands the kid.

The Quality

Between the ice and fire,

Which one is the strongest?

Asked a stranger.

At a random roadside.

And I asked him back.

Which is the fastest?

He, with a confused look.

Me, with a smirk and smile.

"Ice, melts faster

Fire, spreads faster.

Both with equal power

And same intensity.

Yet, differ by

Quality.

Quality of being,"

I mentioned.

And he went on a doubt tour.

"Anything in this world,

Depends.

Depends on its own quality

And

The quality

Decides the very being of the thing."

The Sides

Round the clock,

It was a min for the sky to turn dark,

The sun to set,

And the moon to rise,

Birds to reach the nest,

Flowers to turn dull.

Workers to get back home,

Colleagues to set out for a party,

Students to lock themselves up,

Mothers to start making dinner,

Teens to call,

And lovers to chat.

Within a min,

The day turns upright,

Rest is after the rest – to one side,

Rushing with the fresh – to the other.

Two parts of the world,

Same routine – different timings.

The Bonds

Either the undefined love

Or the defined love,

Which one lasts longer?

Asked a friend of mine.

And I replied,

"Love,

A defined one

By its own."

The friend,

Turned quiet,

And came back

Asking.

Why am I your friend?

What made you my friend?

And I,

Replied.

"The bonds made in the world,

Around the globe

Are built with feelings

and emotions.

To stay in the bond,

If you seek for a reason

You can rather break it

And move on."

Defining a relationship,

Or staying without definition,

Is a personal choice.

Relationships don't seek a reason.

Since they are one.

Connections

In the clear sky,

The birds weren't high,

Midst the clouds and sky,

The sun wasn't hot.

Scattered bubbles,

Reflected rainbow,

At a long distance – a beauty,

Found its happiness.

The pleasing view,

Whipped away her sorrows,

The nature's frankness,

Planted up the confidence.

In the alluring sparkles,

She captured her heartbeat,

Midst the soul and mind,

She captured her longings.

In the clear sky,

She became high,

Midst the conflict and relationship,

The relationship won.

Untamed Fate

Unknown paths,

With sun and moon – back and forth,

With trees and bark – side by side,

At times fragile, at times blooming,

The flowers.

Long run,

With active and tired – mind and heart,

With happiness and sadness – in and out,

At times victory, at times failure,

The games.

Neither narrow nor broad,

With turnings and breaks – speed and slow,

With blocks and clears – here and there,

At times reach, at times cross,

The goals.

Either the point or the destination,

With heart and mind – contentment and pleasure,

With smile and cheer – around and surround,

At times reel, at times real,

The destiny.

Conviction

The longing heart

Craves for more.

The doubtful mind

Double thinks all.

Heart filled with unachievable love,

Mind filled with doubts about doubts,

Heart and mind together,

Together – know the truth.

Yet the trust doubts,

Doubts and craves,

All the time,

Day and night.

What comes even leaves,

What leaves would wish to come,

Yet, it never returns.

The self wouldn't know.

Wouldn't know its insecurity,

What's left would understand,

What stands by will try to understand,

But nothing would satisfy.

As it is insecurity,

Insecurity about the life,

Insecurity in everything,

Insecurity inside the own self.

The Love Left

Ain't your heart too small?

A tiny window may be.

A long time ago,

Love knocked.

But by mistake, let in.

Hatred stepped in.

In a flick peace left,

And was left with ache.

Kindness flew,

Back and forth,

But the string was cut.

And still, love awaited.

As the window,

Missed its key,

Hatred smirked

And filled in glee.

Never to empty,

But the faithful old love,

Naïve and stupid,

Returned and waited.

Erased

The heart would long,

Long to spit out,

Out the dusky past,

Past that's to be erased.

Erased from the unconscious mind.

With the dusky past,

Mind doesn't just ache,

It creates cramps.

Heart overthinks the dusky,

Dusky, not completely bad – yet it is,

It's the broken nature – the sour,

Sour it tastes.

It's the heart that weeps,

Weeps, wept by the conscious,

Conscious joys the heart,

Heart and the inner soul long.

Long at the inner depth,

Depth where the dusky is settled,

Settled with the bed,

Bed of pain, longing for warmth.

The Duet

Turned off the light,

Just to think of the day,

Turned on the mind,

Just to think of the says.

Heart unlocked on its own,

Peeping out with cries,

Soul locked on its own,

Returning in with fears.

Calling them,

Switched on the light,

Directing them,

Mind left with the ray.

Emotions entered with hurt,

Feelings knocked with scars,

To fold or unfold?

"Instinct" – wasn't bold.

Mind left without train,

Collapsed instinct stood – in the battle,

Battle between,

Heart and mind.

An Escapism

Between the long barks,

The earthy green – a fresh aura

Between the confused branches,

The ray of sun – a bright one

Between the hanging tenders,

The childish feeling – a longing one,

Between the trees,

The lengthy road – a forever one,

Between the tips,

The never-ending feel – an escapism.

The Rage

The rage in her eyes,

The bloody tears that fell,

As she was told: "Behave yourself,"

The rose like a tender heart,

Grew its thorns,

As it leaned over the rock,

To become one.

The Pause

In the midst of the chaos,

All the heart needed

Was a moment.

To hold on and relax.

Why would you wait? – The brain asked.

 "The pause is a need now" – the heart replied

The boiling anger must be let out – the brain
reverted.

And the heart ignored.

The heart stayed in silence.

As the rage calmed down,

It feels its life.

The moment is what it views – now.

Heart looks around

And feels its own self – now.

All it could feel, after all this

Is a sorry

The moment takes a turn,

The chaos loses its grip.

And all that's left

Is love.

The moment of pause

Calmed down the rage

And bloomed

The love.

The Silver Lining

There are quite a lot of times when,

Things wouldn't fall at right place.

But what matters is,

When it does fall,

Without a second thought,

The heart should accept it.

Deserving

At the end,

All that stays is

What remains.

At the close,

All that remains is

What prevails.

What remains

And

What prevails

Is all that.

That deserves to be

Until the death.

The Hopeful Bud

A little bud,

With an enchanting sparkle on its sides,

With a very skinny, tender,

Yet a strong stem,

Makes you wait for – a sweet bloom,

The bloom that washes away the sadness.

A little hope,

With eternal happiness on its soul,

With confidence on one part,

Yet doubt engulfing the other side,

Makes you wait for its destiny,

The destiny that fades away or fades in.

The Nature's Call

Knees clutched as she sat,

With fiery eyes,

That bled with tears,

The breeze was harsh,

The thunder hit hard,

Harder than she thought,

The power was on and off,

The windows called her,

Called her to show the – other side,

Another side of the world,

The long she refused –
The long she missed the peaceful heaven.

Heaven – where the breeze turned romantic,

where the flowers would sway along the breeze,

where the drizzles would kiss her cheeks,

where the knees would be unclutched and left to roam,

where the hands would swing,

 and the feet would break dance,

Altogether,

The nature would wipe her tears,

And the scenic world would heal her.

The more she sat, the more she missed.

The more she regrets, the more she locks,

The more it thunders, the more she hides.

The harsh call

Strikes hard

To bring her out,

Yet, she locks herself.

I Wish I Could Be

I wish I could be a cloud,

As I want to be

Pure and fluffy with the blue sky,

Dark and contented with the starry sky,

Consistent with the change

Scattered with the range.

I wish I could be one among all.

As I long to be

Bright in the day,

Dimmed in the night,

Alive all the time,

Popping out when in need.

Into the Meadow

Into the meadows,

Below the slaying sun,

Between the weathering purple petals,

She found a life.

A life which made her swirl,

Swirl like Rapunzel,

With her

Long magical, golden hair.

The rays of light,

On her bright face,

Her big round eyes,

Shut, to feel.

She deeply swirled

In the magic of the moment,

With fresh breaths

And serenity.

The birds singing around,

The clouds stilling above,

The greens and purples below,

And she.

She and the moment

Was all in her heart.

The meadows,

Mended her.

The Work Routine

When the sun was about to set,

When the clouds were about to leave,

When the birds were around the nest,

When the roads were all set.

All the soul wanted was a peaceful,

A peaceful ride.

With the breezy evening,

The soul wanted a long ride.

Without a destination,

It was all set.

Without a thought,

It was all set.

Why would I want to go out?

The soul didn't question.

Was it tired or was it exhausted?

The soul didn't know.

The packed routine,

The round-the-clock job,

The submissions and deadlines.

The work life.

Was the soul packed by that?

The loss of me time,

The ignorance of family time,

The avoiding of friends' time.

Did the soul feel bad about it?

The soul didn't know anything

Other than the breezy evening.

The soul longed for the mental peace.

The ride along the wind,

The acceleration toward an unknown destination,

When even the loneliness felt like happiness,

The soul breathed in and out.

The soul realized, At times:

The unlonged happenings.

The unplanned sudden rides.

Let the soul breathe.

Chaos of Thought

With the flowing river,

Flowed his thoughts.

The tall, introverted guy

At the river side.

Nothing around him,

Mattered to him,

All he was staring at

Was the flowing water.

Without a tilt,

He was all into it.

The deep river,

And he.

Without a blink,

He was sinked

Into the chaos.

The chaos of thoughts.

The Doubt

A long way,

A long run,

What matters – I doubt,

Strongly.

The speed or the patience,

The will power or the determination,

The competitor or the betterment,

The hope or the belief.

Everything seems

To be covered

Under the same umbrella.

But still, I doubt.

The sun and moon

Always glow,

Glow without

Any end.

What makes them glow?

The philosophy or the science?

The strength or the confidence?

What makes it to the goal?

Is it

The hard work or the consistency?

The talent or the acquired talent?

The dream or the luck?

I stand at the same place,

At the same phase,

With the doubt.

Doubt of what matters.

The Over Thinking

If it seems simple,

Why it feels complex?

If it seems easy,

Why it feels hard,

If it seems clear,

Why it feels opaque,

If it seems vague,

Why doesn't it feel okay?

It's actually,

How it is.

It isn't pretending,

And ain't complicating.

The thought and

The perception,

Are what causes.

Causes – the over thinking.

The Girl Under the Orange Light

The girl under the orange light,

Hid herself in the dark,

Her broken heart,

In the scary night.

Her shattered dream,

within her loud screams,

Her unspoken words,

Seldom heard.

Her hidden enthusiasm,

In the world's sarcasm,

Her half-woven life,

In the tip of a knife.

Her scribbles – Her poems.

Her sorrows – the rhythm,

Her scars – the words.

And she – the poet,

The girl under the orange light,

Destined the destiny night.

The Guiding Street Lights in the Dark

Beneath the random streetlights,

Pulling the sweater tight,

Hugging myself,

Through the darkness,

I was.

Random guys racing in the street,

Laughing at me with the bottles,

Smoke from the flame nearing me,

Neither my eyes felt drained,

Nor my soul broke.

Beneath the random streetlight,

Smiling at the happening,

Cherishing the weather,

Through the rays of moon,

I drove.

Random guys gulping in the mid,

Staring at me they winked,

Losing their mind, they were,

Neither had I felt weird,

Nor I searched for shelter.

Beneath the random streetlight,

Exploring the paths,

Experiencing the loneliness,

Through the peace,

I flew.

Mistakes

The anger it evoked,

The patience I lost,

To listen – I refused,

To follow – I said a big no.

The pity I felt,

The value it gained,

To stay quiet – I decided,

To never disturb – it finalized.

The low I felt,

Everywhere it stood front,

Not to prove itself,

To make me realize.

Mistakes, I made

A boring song,

Yet, a temporary hurt

And a permanent happiness.

Wish

Wish I could tell someone,

How hurt I am.

Wish I could pour out,

My darkest truths.

Wish I could dump,

All the longings.

Wish I could silence,

All the screams.

Wish I would smile,

Genuinely.

Wish I would fly,

Happily.

Wish I keep a full stop,

To the inner cravings.

Wish I could keep a track,

Of my inner soul.

Wish my heart,

Fills with vibes.

Wish my eyes,

Fill with cherries.

Wish my unspoken words,

Be spelled.

Wish my un-spelled words,

Be said.

Wish my deepest fears,

Be gone.

Wish my darkest nights,

Be lit.

Memories

I still remember those random childhood days,

The days which passed by ease,

The days which were lit, and had light,

The days which were filled by golden rays.

Far away,

Nah! Not that far away,

Just far yet not so distant,

The days filled with love and life.

I still remember those random childhood days,

When I clinged on to you,

When I roamed everywhere with you,

When I was surrounded by you.

It's been years,

Yet no distance,

It's been a long way,

Yet no wave.

I still remember those random childhood days,

The days which had the day and night,

The days which had the says and pays,

The days which had the we and us.

We,

We have grown up

To your height,

Yet, we remain the same young kids.

Young kids,

With height.

Young kids,

To you.

I still remember those random childhood days,

With all the ups and downs,

And likes and dislikes,

Still, the heart holds.

She, An Unknown Poetry

Her eyes always smiled,

Her lips – always wide,

Her face always glowing,

Her laugh – always mesmerizing.

She, always around,

Striving hard,

Her pain – no one knew of,

Her craving – no one cared for.

Her heart never spoke out,

Her soul – always in peace,

Her mind always positive,

Her – acceptance – no one would know.

She, an unknown poetry,

Filled with love,

Her success – everyone knows,

Her dream – everyone wonders.

Hope is Alive

Though your heart is aching,

Though your inner soul is suffering,

Though your intuition failed you,

Though your mind gave up on you.

Though your prediction took off,

Though your perception went wrong,

Though your opinion didn't win,

Though your expectation didn't happen.

Though your close ones left you,

Though your dream broke down,

Though your goal is too far,

Though your life is stuck.

Smile.

Turns

115

Things take turns,

Not a slight turn,

Either an inverted

Or a spiral one.

How does it take?

With a brake or

Within a break?

Humans think.

But lose everything within a wink,

Everything wouldn't become pink,

Either black or white,

Nothing gray in-between.

They lose or win,

They give up or take it down,

They move on or move out,

They think or forget.

Some,

Some stay and wait,

Wait with all the heart,

Wait with so much of positivity.

But at the end,

That few,

Lose.

Lose everything.

The turn,

Yeah, that one!

Is it necessary?

Does it show something?

A lesson or a memory,

A pain or a mask,

Anything,

But it shows.

Shows the value,

Makes us—

Realize.

Thus, things take turns.

The Fall

If the fall will

Gives you wings

With a will,

Will you doubt your fall?

If the fall will

Give you wings

With abundant strength,

Will you fear your fall?

If the fall will

Give you wings

With better luck,

Will you curse your fall?

If the fall will

Tighten your grip

With immense confidence,

Will you worry about your fall?

If the fall will

grip your hold

With inner peace,

Will you rant about your fall?

If the fall will

Plant a new way

With flowers and stars,

Will you step back from the fall?

If the fall will

Bring your destiny

With great success,

Will you fight with your fall?

If the fall

Is where you

Raise back stronger,

Why don't you fall again and again?

To Go with Flow

Things fold,

Yet, matters unfold.

Truth breaks,

Yet, lies stay.

Plans happen,

Yet, over-planning fails.

Dreams pave way,

Yet, goals so far away.

Darkness ends,

Yet, days go on.

Problems sort out,

Yet, conflicts happen.

Expectation ends,

Yet, acceptance never happens.

Flow matters,

Yet, go with the flow,

Travel is long,

Yet, go slow.

Distance matters,

Yet don't give up.

The Destination

As I sat between the trees and bushes,

Empty pathway and road before me,

In a string chair,

With the heart soothing wind.

I was thinking about,

The inner peace.

There was a man,

Who questioned me –

"What's in my mind?"
"What's inner peace?"

I answered him there.

But now, I think, Was I right?

The soul with no past baggage,

With no grudge or intention for revenge,

With no ego and

without why me questions,

Is the soul with inner peace I answered there.

Does a soul exist in this world?

With inner peace,

With calm mind,

If one does,

Then that's the soul,

The only soul,

Which is living in the present.

Romanticizing with nature,

Admiring the beings,

Smiling at the randomers,

Laughing at the lame jokes,

Playing with the kinds,

Flirting with the opposites,

They aren't inner peace,

They are just the moment's peace.

Inner peace is the ultimate,

The destination— Ultimate Destination.

The Heart

The heart stays with the hurt,

The hurt develops the grudge,

The grudge longs for the revenge,

The revenge stops "the peace."

The pieces flip off,

The happiness awaits,

The longings fly away,

Ego starts "the rule."

The soul bids smile,

The tears find place,

The heart tears apart,

The attitude waves "the welcome."

The hurt stays,

Not as a tenant,

Fueling the heart,

Firing the soul.

The Peace

Since I was flying,

The roads and the passages,

The houses and the huts,

The temples and the worshiping places,

The restaurants and theaters,

Were left out of the view

What was left to me yet?

The fluffy clouds and the bare sky,

With nothing, yet a pleasing view,

With the ray of light,

Passing through the clouds,

The sky glows.

The bare sky,

The empty one,

Yet, the peace.

The Heart in Peace

As I stood at the top of a hill,

With the clouds still,

Calm and chill,

The sun.

The sun was,

Close to my fingers,

With its golden rays on,

The heat was low but the mood.

The mood was joy,

As the nature became a toy,

Violets and pinks surround,

What else do I search or feel or dream or scream?

What else?

Nothing pops up,

Neither in my mind nor

In my heart – contented? Nah! In peace.

The Known Dream

The ends of the paths,

Are unknown,

The hurdles in the paths,

Are unknown,

The turnings in the way,

Are unknown,

The rides in the way,

Are unknown.

The feelings that pass,

Are unknown,

The characters that pass,

Are unknown,

The destiny is unknown,

Yet, the dream is known.

The Dream Land

Though it was an imaginary land,

Pretended to be

Better than the

Disney Land.

It was a beautiful heart gulfing vision,

Unrealistic yet,

A charming,

Imagination.

A colorful garden with heart throbbing,

Flowers. Flower Garden

Seemed to be

A garland of love.

Pretty flowers stacked in an

Unordered order,

Creating a

Soothing sight.

Though the dream,

Would disappear soon,

The occupied mind

Wished to Live.

Wished to stand in

The passage,

Looking at the

Unordered yet, ordered flowers.

The roses,

The tulips,

The daffodils,

The daisies.

The morning glories,

The sunflowers,

The spearmints,

The rosemaries.

Was all

That the mind could keep,

And dream and keep on dreaming.

The imaginary land – The dream.

To The Lonely Ones

By the way,

Writing to the lonely ones,

Neither you are alone,

Nor you are experiencing loneliness,

Either you were left alone,

Or you make yourself alone,

Neither you are broken,

Nor you break yourself alone.

Either your expectations were killed,

Or you over-expected.

Nothing remains the same,

Everything changes,

Either time will heal,

Or you will heal,

Neither people will forgive,

Nor you will forgive,

Either the left ones will enter,

Or new ones will do,

Neither have they deserved second chance,

Nor you deserve.

In This Universe

In this universe,

Where you can't reverse,

Reverse anything,

Not even a string.

In this universe,

Where you can be a story,

Story of fate,

Which can't be remade.

In this universe,

Where you can't handle,

Handle emotions,

Not even a single night.

In this universe,

Where you can be an inspiration,

Inspiration to the beings,

Which can be history.

In this universe,

Where you can't tackle a rumor,

Rumor like a wildfire,

Not even a minute.

In this universe,

Where everything is freedom,

Freedom is free,

Which can be held.

In this universe,

Where you are granted,

Granted everything,

Be you.

A Short Note to My Beautiful Readers

If you have reached this point of my book, I am seriously blessed to have a reader like you.

Never forget,

You have got two choices in life:

One is to worry and stress yourself

And the other is to smile as much as you can and chill.

Choose to be HAPPY…

Be A Sunshine!

www.ingramcontent.com/pod-product-compliance
Lightning Source LLC
Chambersburg PA
CBHW031629170726
47990CB00017B/424